Crossroads
A Guide for Finding Your Path

STEVE SPUR

AVERY
PUBLISHING

Copyright © 2013 Steve Spur

All rights reserved.

ISBN: 0615791301
ISBN-13: 978-0615791302

DEDICATION

This book is dedicated to:

my loving wife PJ

my daughters Meagan and Sara

my granddaughter Avery

You make this journey and my life worth living.

CONTENTS

	Preface	i
1	In a Nutshell	1
2	Finding Your Path	12
3	Make a Difference	24
4	Guiding Light	31
5	Opening Up	37
6	Just Breathe	49
7	Imagine	55
8	Recommended Reading	62

PREFACE

I don't believe in accidents, chance or coincidences. Everything is synchronized and happens at the proper place and time. Now you may be asking yourself, "Who am I? or, Why am I here?" You may be asking, "What is my life's purpose?" and "Is this all there is to life? There has to be something else!" It's not about making the most money and collecting the most wealth, because you can't take it with you. Somehow, you knew that already. Some of you are a little scared and you fear change, while others have an empty space in your heart that needs to be filled with love. Let me assure you that everything you have ever done in your life has been to get you to this point in your life, which I refer to as The Crossroads.

You are starting to wake up and shed a little of your ego. Suddenly it's not all about you. So you don't have it all figured out? That's great, because nobody does! You are starting to change the way you think and starting to stick your head out of your shell and look around. I can tell you that you have done no wrong in your life and your past was made up of a bunch of interesting experiences to get you ready for your soul's purpose. I was skeptical at first, too!

I am a skeptic. I wasn't a particularly spiritual or religious person until the day that I fell from the sky (the attic) and down the "rabbit hole" to the concrete. Ever since that day, I've been on a path to help as many people as possible. Some people called it a near death experience. Later, I would call it an awakening. After the accident, I began to hear and see dead people. It turns out they have a lot to say. The future is not set in stone. Every day begins and ends with endless possibilities; each road leads to a thousand paths and you can choose to take any one of them: the road less traveled, the safe road, or a path of your own choosing.

It's not enough just to know there is another side, that most people call heaven, and I've proved it to thousands of people. So how do you live your life knowing you can't die? Oh, you can die in this world, but not in the next!

Why are you here? What do you want? I always ask people "If you had every material thing in the world and all of the money that you needed, would you be happy?" Watch out, materialism is a trap! Could you really enjoy yourself with all of the suffering in the world? Get back on track. Why did you come down here? Don't tell me you didn't choose this life and time, because I can prove that you did.

You came to this dimension and time to learn certain lessons. This is part of your evolution or soul learning. You want to learn so you can grow. As you grow, you can help others. You are enrolled in Earth School. You can't drop out, because you'll just send yourself back.

Nobody made you come to Earth School. That's okay because you didn't come alone. You have a Master Guide, helper guides, a Guardian Angel, as well as your Soul Group helping you! You have a safety net and you can't fail in this lifetime. You heard me right! If you don't learn your lessons in this lifetime, you will in the next or the next, or you can find your path, stay on it, and learn as much as you can in this lifetime and move upward and onward. The choice is yours. You can swim upstream against the current or get out of the water and walk up the gentle hill to find your purpose. Someone should write a simply worded guide for the millions of people who are awakening each day and want to distance themselves from their self-imposed illusions and find their path.

IN A NUTSHELL

When the one great scorer comes to write against your name, he marks, not that you won or lost, but how you played the game.

—Grantland Rice

What's it all about? I still don't have it all figured out yet. Anyone who says that they have all the answers is a liar! I've seen it all and done half of it. However, I can tell you that you have a choice. I wished I'd known what I know now, thirty years ago! I'm just going to tell you like it is, no lies. I don't have a reason to lie. I've been lied to all of my life by people who didn't know any better. I forgive them. Yes, it is difficult to forgive, at least for me. You have to forgive to progress down the path to the pleasures that await you! However, I'm getting ahead of myself. Most of the stuff I'm writing about blew my mind. It took me a long time to accept it. It doesn't matter if you believe what I'm saying or not! Just keep the concepts in the back of your mind; you'll hear them repeatedly by others as you progress on your journey!

Without giving a physics lesson, certain physicists came up with M-theory, an extension of string theory that says there could be at least 11 dimensions in this world. Okay, so we live in one of these dimensions, and there is another place I call the other side and that some people call heaven, that is in our dimension only separated by a thin two-way mirror. That's all I need to know right now. In this universe, there are millions of suns and tens of millions of other planets and it goes on and on. I just try to concentrate on the 100-some-odd square feet around me at any one time. So, I can tell you that you were somewhere else before you came to this world or dimension. You didn't have a physical body, but did and still do have a soul. Energy can't be destroyed, and your soul is energy!

Your soul is in paradise, so why in the hell would anyone want to come down to this harsh environment called Earth? You have to come here to grow. You have to have experiences to grow. On the other side, there are only pleasant experiences such as, happiness, love, joy, bliss, satisfaction, peace and hope. Now, many of those experiences are available on Earth. However, at what depths can you feel love, joy, bliss and peace if you haven't experienced their opposites? We have to come down here to experience pain, suffering, greed, agony, lies, illness, worry, anguish, heartache, misery, grief, anxiety, stress, discomfort, hurt, sorrow, disappointment, trouble, depression, and death. Not everyone signs up for all of the experiences in this lifetime. Others are going for it all. You can also learn from other people's experiences. I don't have to live through a debilitating disease to feel compassion for the people who are going through it. Here's the kicker, we all have gone through everything throughout history and throughout our existence as a soul.

That's right, I've killed you and you've killed

me. I've been a woman and a man and have had every color of skin you can imagine. This concept blew my tiny little brain and it still does at times. I talk to dead people. I ask them, "Where are you?" and they answer, "On the other side!" I also ask, "Will I see you again?" they always answer, "Yes." I'm not the only one who had a problem with reincarnation. One of the greatest psychic mediums who ever lived, Edgar Cayce, had a problem with it. You see, he wanted to be a preacher and he read the entire Bible, for every year he was alive. He didn't think the Bible talked about reincarnation. However, if you pretend for a second that there is reincarnation and Jesus believed in it and reread the Bible you may find it very interesting and that's what changed Edgar Cayce's mind. You can look it up yourself.

My wife is a hypnotist who regresses (hypnotizes) people back to past lives and life between lives (heaven). She studied with the foremost authorities about past lives and life between lives. There are a ton of books available about children who remember their past lives as well. (There is a list for

Recommended Reading in the back of the book.) If you've come this far on your journey, I think you are open minded enough to accept the possibility of reincarnation. Just keep the possibility in the back of your mind.

On the other side, before you incarnate to Earth you have some very wise souls who want to help you and who can give you advice. I call these wise old ones the Council of Elders. I have a Master Spirit Guide who has been with me for countless incarnations who helps me when I ask for help and you have a Spirit Guide too. I also have a Soul Group made up of between fifteen and twenty-five souls that I work with. They are all my Soul Mates, who play the roles of friends and family in my different incarnations. We have a shopping list of things we want to learn in a lifetime. We talk it over with our elders, guides and other souls in the group. It's like casting for a movie. I'll be your kid who gets killed in a war in this life. You'll be my wife in the next, a grandfather in the next and so on. Everyone helps everyone on the other side. There is no judgment;

there is only love and understanding!

We all have free will, but more than likely the events that surround you in this life were of your own making. Remember all of the things you can't experience in heaven. I can watch someone die and see the people grieving for them, but if I haven't experienced a loved one dying myself, then it's an experience that I haven't had and can't comprehend. You see where I'm going with this? You know you don't have to have a medium available to talk to your loved ones, Spirit Guides or angels. When I started figuring this stuff out, I had a long talk with my Master Guide and it started something like this, "What the hell was I thinking and why didn't you talk me out of this?"

Now there are a lot of frauds and con artists out there, and I see them all the time. When I talk to your dead relatives and loved ones, I don't want general information like, "Your grandmother is coming through and she loves and misses you." Hell, you already knew that. I want concrete evidence, like "I have your grandmother Nelly coming through. She says she had a cat called Frankie and was married to Bill in Louisville, Kentucky, where he worked at Churchill Downs and he died on July 17th." You see where I'm going? Is there any doubt now that I'm talking to your grandmother? I don't want you to have any doubt. Sometimes, they'll tell me that your back tire on the passenger's side is too low on your car or that you need to quit smoking so you can continue on your path.

My Spirit Guides have a lot of patience. My Guardian Angel is one badass dude! They all must be working off some major karma to be assigned to me. So let's talk about that karma that I'll be working off the rest of this life and maybe many more. It's not that I killed anyone in this life. However, maybe I wasn't a model citizen. Energy can't be destroyed. Energy can't be good or bad, it just is. Your body and mind remember everything in every life that you have ever lived. There is a reason we don't remember our past lives. If I were to remember what you did to me in the last life, well I may not be as advanced as I think I am and reap a little revenge. In the next life, you remember my revenge and so on. When would it ever stop? However, if I did something negative to you that you didn't ask for, well then I'd owe a debt to you (karma) that I need to repay. Maybe I can do something good for someone else in this life and pay you back, and the bad deed can be taken off the books. Those books are called the Akashic Records and everything that you ever did and everything that has been done is in the book. The next time you're on the other side, drop by the library and look it up. It will knock your socks off!

Okay, so you have a game plan coming down here. Your angels are going to keep you safe until it's your time to die. I forgot to mention that you also arranged your death. It sounds wild, but did you really think these things happen at random at this point in the handbook? It works like this: You and your guides agree that you will live twenty-five years in this life and that you would like to die in a murder. You see that there are a few people left in your Soul Group who haven't experienced a murder of a loved one, so you'll work it in that they are part of your family in this incarnation. You agree to help everyone in your Soul Group and you check out at twenty-five years of age. It really doesn't matter if you're shot, in a car wreck or natural disaster. It may just be what's easiest at the time. Have you ever noticed how many people die just after a birthday or Christmas? Surely, you don't believe in coincidences at this time in your life. There are no coincidences or chance. There is a reason for everything. That's why you have guides and angels to help you. If it weren't for them, you'd never learn your lessons or find your Soul Mate.

Have you ever experienced déjà vu? Did it scare you just a little? Did you ever have a feeling or vision that you've experienced something before or have been in this exact place, but you know that you haven't? What do you think it was? Was it a past life? You are already cast in this movie we'll call, "My Life." You know what part you'll play, the things you've got to do and the rest of the cast. However, how you play it is up to you. You can cast a hundred different people for the same movie and you'll end up with a hundred different versions. Did everyone die when they were supposed to? You bet they did, but it was a different movie from yours. It isn't predestination because you have free will. If it hadn't been for free will, I'd be a helluva lot more advanced now! If I'd just listened to my intuition (Higher Self) and angels and guides, I'd be done with my lessons or at the very least, a lot more advanced. Ego gets in the way. You're a legend in your own mind! Déjà vu is like a tiny breadcrumb to guide you on the path. You were shown scenes in this lifetime before you came down here. You can act out the scene however you like, but you have an idea of how it should go on the other side. That's what your guides and angels showed you and that's what you're seeing or feeling with déjà vu. It's one brick of the yellow brick road. You are on your path!

Earlier, I mentioned your Higher Self. This is your soul, or the part that stays in heaven. You see another part of your soul is on the other side, always has been and always will be. Your soul is on the other side right now and part of it is in your body. Some people like to call it your Higher Self. The goal is to synchronize your Lower Self (ego) with the Higher Self, your soul. Believe me, it's easier said than done. I'll bet there are but a handful of people walking the globe who are at this point. If they are, they are here to set examples and teach. Watch a bunch of eighteen-month old children sometime. They go around kissing each other sharing their toys (until they turn two) and are living in the moment and enjoying it all. They'll fall down and get back up because they don't know that it isn't part of daily life. It's only when mom runs over to them and kisses them and tells them it's all right that they figure out that it's not okay to fall down. Living in the moment, enjoying the better things in life and learning from the bad, that's what I'm talking about. Are you with me? Haven't trashed the book yet? Great, let's get on with finding your true path!

FINDING YOUR PATH

I have learned this at least by my experiments: that if one advances confidently in the direction of his dreams and endeavors to live the life which he has imagined, he will meet with a success unexpected in common hours.

—Henry David Thoreau

Your life may be at a crossroads now. You don't feel comfortable doing and living your life. You know there is something out there that is more fulfilling! Why do you want to change your life? Your ego doesn't. However, if you're reading this, you already have started. I'm always open to suggestions and hope to have an open mind. What would you do if you had everything in the world that you needed? Got enough money? How much is enough? Does having enough money change the way you listen to music, look at the beauty in the world? So you don't do everything in this lifetime, save a little for the next. The biggest thing in finding your path is changing the way you think. I didn't say it would be easy, but with practice, anything can be achieved. When I was a young man, I wanted to be an Olympic boxer or swimmer and win the Kentucky Derby. Did I? No, but I sure learned a lot trying. Don't trust anyone! Don't tell anyone your dreams unless they can help you achieve them! It's all a state of mind. Don't be a hater. It takes years to overcome. Open your mind to the possibilities!

What makes you feel good? Drugs, cigarettes, alcohol, food, sex or money, it's all an illusion! You can dream about these things without experiencing them and still feel the same. The dream doesn't have all of the consequences of some of those experiences. What if I told you that you could experience anything physical or mental at the snap of your fingers? We'll get to that. I didn't say it would be easy. First, think about cutting back on the excesses in your life so you can spend more time doing what really matters to you. How do you know what really matters to you if you haven't experienced everything yet? Play along for just a little while.

Get a piece of paper and make a list. We'll call this the "Wish List." Write down all of the things that you would like to experience, or think you might want to. Some people call this the "bucket list" or things you'd like to do before you kick the bucket. It may just be goals for the future, such as jobs, life partners, etc.

Next, make another list. This is your "Happy List." Write all of the things that have made you happy from the time you can remember as a baby to the present. If it makes you happy when someone smiles at you, write it down. If it makes you happy when your favorite song comes on the radio, write it down.

Okay, now make a third list of all of the things you have done in your life to make other people happy. This is your, "Good Deeds List." Did you teach or coach anyone to help them reach a goal? Were you kind or nice to someone? Write it down. Now all of these lists may take a while, maybe weeks.

When you get the lists in front of you, start looking for some of the things they may have in common. Some of the things that you did for other people may also have made you happy, so they are on the second and third list. Look at all of the things that have made you happy and add to that all of the people in your life who helped you feel happy.

I love ice cream. Someone had to make the ice cream and someone at the ice cream store scooped out my ice cream and sold it to me. I'm thankful for the whole lot of people who made that scoop of ice cream possible. It was worth every penny I spent on it and I hope every cent will go to those who helped make this ice cream possible for me, so that they may spend it on something I love as much as ice cream. It feels like Karma.

So now make a "Grateful List," of every little and big thing you are grateful for, from the clothes on your back, the food in the refrigerator, to the person who wrote your favorite song or movie. It used to be, I wasn't grateful for much. I didn't care about anyone else, just living in my own selfish, little hateful world. Sometimes, it takes someone to point out the beautiful things in the world, such as all of the opportunities that you've had it this life and how much of your life you may have wasted. I can tell you right here and now, don't look back! The past is literally history; it is spilled milk that can never be returned to the bottle. Don't spend one second of the rest of your life regretting anything. There is a reason for everything. We may not know those reasons until we get to the other side or until we grow enough as people, so that we can see the bigger picture! You have to forgive yourself as well as others. It leads to unconditional love! I didn't say it would be easy to forgive yourself or others. Think about it this way. Say a little two-year-old child just broke your most precious possession. Are you going to hold that against them the rest of their life? Of course, you won't. Why? Because they don't know any better. The child is not as evolved as you are. You are not as evolved as you think you are and there are millions of souls who forgive you on this side and the other. Pay it forward and give the unevolved the benefit of the doubt.

Now let's take a test. You'll like this test. Take something from your list of things you'd like to experience, from your "Wish List," that you think would make you happy. Think about it. Are you skydiving or watching the sunrise at the Grand Canyon? Shut your eyes and daydream about it. We call this visualization. This is the way your loved ones and relatives come to me when I'm giving a reading. It's like watching a movie in my head, one that they put there. It's not enough just to visualize this event. How does it feel? What are the physical sensations? What are the mental sensations? You feel it, taste it, smell it, hear it and see it. Do you feel the smile on your face? Isn't it great? Did you feel it with all of your heart and soul? Did you get a little déjà vu, as if maybe you already experienced this in another lifetime? It's something to think about.

So it felt good. I call this visualization:

meditating. Wow! So that's meditating. You got a thrill, your mind and body got a rest and you are in a better place having experienced it. That's right; you can do that with anything. Your mind does it at night two or more times, when you are dreaming. Yes, everyone dreams; you just don't remember them all. If you want to remember what your subconscious dreams are about, put it on your list. I'm serious as a heart attack. It works! Take a deep breath next time and it helps the process. Take steady, even, deep breaths and it gives your mind something to do while you're experiencing paradise.

So now you have a handy tool to change your life and get on a different path! Get out another piece of paper and take the number one item on your wish list. So, you want to climb Mount Everest, great! Let's make a list of everything that needs to happen for you to do this. Number one, you're going to need equipment. Go on climbing websites and read climbing books and write down what you're going to need in the way of supplies. You're going to need a guide or to join a group that has a little experience doing this, so start researching. You're going to need a plane ticket and a vacation from your job. You may not be making enough money at your current job, so if this is really important to you, you may take a second job.

However, you really hate your present job. Okay, put that on the list. I want a better job, one that I like to do and one where I enjoy working with people who I like. Okay, not all of us have that luxury to get a great job at the drop of a hat. However, I can change how I feel about the job that is helping me make enough money to climb Everest! Wow, I never thought about it that way. Remember the little visualization you did? Now use it at work so you're not doing mindless tasks, but you're climbing the mountain now. How does it feel? Pretty damn good!

Climbing lessons! You're going to need climbing lessons. Okay, add it all up and put your list in order of the things you need to do first; prioritize the list. This is your blueprint for achieving your goal of climbing Mt. Everest! You have just added a branch to the path you are experiencing. It is number one on your list of things you want to do (Wish List) and number one on the things that would make me happy list (Happy list). Where is it on the Helping Other People List? Would it be even better if you could share the experience and help some other people who have the same goal but don't know how to go about it? Yeah, sure it would. Helping some kids who may be considered handicapped by others? Maybe someone who is dying and this would be their last chance to climb?

You have the key in your hand. All of the answers are on those sheets of paper. You can do it anytime you want. Let's say you go ahead and do it. You climbed Everest! How did it feel? Pretty good! Soak up the joy. You accomplished something really special. Congratulations! Do you want to do it again? Was it a fluke that you made your goal on the first try? Do you need to set a world record to feel you've accomplished something? Can it get any better? You bet it can. Share the joy! Teach someone else how to do it. Serve someone else so they can share the joy. Wow! This deal just got sweeter! I can increase my joy and pleasure times one hundred, times one thousand, by helping others. Oh my God, it's not all about me! You just evolved to another level. Your soul just experienced another awakening! I've wasted so much time in this life! Learn from the past, enjoy the present and evolve for the future!

So if you think that your "Good Deeds List" and your "Gratitude list" is more important than your "Wish List" then you get it! You've graduated from one of the classes in Earth School. It turns out that making other people happy and the things you are grateful for now make up the list that makes you happy and gives your life purpose. That's why you came down to Earth School to learn. Jesus, Buddha, Mohamed, Crazy Horse and all of the great masters taught it and lived it. Not everyone is ready to be in the class that you're in. Not everyone is ready to awaken and evolve to your level. I don't judge a first grader because he doesn't speak three languages and understand calculus yet. In time, if that is his or her path, they will learn those things in this lifetime. I'll save the calculus for another life.

Get all of your lists together and figure out your path for this life. You think you came up with those lists all by yourself? I'm not that smart! Your guides and angels put those ideas in your head. They inspire you. They nudge you to work or meet a certain person. They give you an idea to go to a certain motivational movie or to buy a book that you had no idea how much you'd enjoy. There is no chance! Everything is synchronistic. Your life is too important not to have meaning! Why did this happen to me or why didn't that happen? At some stage in your existence, it will all become clear. Nobody has all of the answers. However, you do have enough answers to keep you moving forward on your path!

At some point in your life, you need to live, experience life, figure out what it's about and live life to its fullest. At the same point in this life, you need to experience love! You need to experience any kind and every kind of love. While you are living and loving, you are learning. This is a cycle in your life. It's all about you. It may be a little selfish, but we all learn this at different stages in our lifecycle. Once you've experienced everything that you've wanted to, and have learned and loved, what else is there? I go back to my gratitude list and see that I've had it pretty good. I'm alive and well. I'm at a point on my path that I'm looking for an intersection, a crossroads that I can take to learn and feel something different. I'm ready to evolve in this life. Is there anything in this world to do?

MAKE A DIFFERENCE

Treat people as if they were what they ought to be and you help them to become what they are capable of being.

—**Goethe**

Looking back on my life, I think I was pretty selfish at times. But that's okay. If I didn't know how it was to be selfish, I wouldn't know how good it feels to share! Hey, maybe that's a life lesson I have to learn in every life in Earth School. You have to start somewhere!

Kindergarten and first grade is a good place to start. Don't look down the road to see how far you have left. Look back and see how far you've come. I took my first step today. Tomorrow I'm going to take a second step and double my progress! You live, love and learn. Then, you teach, serve and evolve.

It's such an easy game! You can never fail! You can never sin! Failure and sin is an illusion to keep you locked up and under control. Drop the invisible chains that bind you and free your mind. It doesn't matter if you are poor or even in prison. Drop your self-imposed limitations. No one is handicapped, although we are all challenged and it's of our own making. It was part of the plan. I have a hard time wrapping my mind around it, but it's true!

Nothing gives me more joy than giving a reading to someone and proving to them, with information that only they can validate, that their loved ones are on the other side and can see and hear everything they do. They share in your joy and pain. Your loved ones are not dead and you can't die. It is so refreshing to understand this concept and have it proven to you. What did your loved ones who have crossed over learn in this life? Whose lives did they change for the better? What did they teach? What did you learn from them, unconditional love or patience?

What can you pass on to someone else?

Everything happens for a reason. I don't believe in predestination, but I do believe that we knew some of the situations that we might meet before we came down here. I believe déjà vu is a short glimpse of some of the places and situations that we were shown so we know we are on the right track. I also believe we work with the same people life after life. The close group of people you work with are in your Soul Group. This group may be made up of between fifteen and thirty people. You work with them time and time again. I'm your son in one life, your father in the next. I'm the daughter, wife, sister, grandparent, best friend, coach, teacher, etc. Think of the twenty most influential people in your life so far. Chances are they are probably in your Soul Group.

Every one we work with is a teacher. The people you love and the people you hate are teachers. You can learn something from everyone! You never stop learning and growing. You are also a teacher. People watch you and learn from you. Do you have a pleasant personality? Are you happy, loving and giving? Are you too shy to talk to people? Are you too weak to change the environment around you? I doubt it. Everyone on this planet has a purpose! You are either a teacher or a student at any given time. I had a friend ask me what color belt I had in Kung Fu. I told him we didn't have belts in our school. You either kicked ass or had your ass kicked. At any given time, you are a teacher or a student, no belts.

You may ask "What do I have that I can teach someone or how can I change someone's life for the better?" More than likely, you weren't meant to change as many lives as Jesus, Mohammad or Buddha, although, I could be wrong. You may be a parent with one child and your only mission in this lifetime is to provide love and be a positive role model for this child. As you help him find his path, he may be the next great teacher! You may work as a server at a restaurant and have a difficult time making ends meet. You do the best you can with what you have and try to keep it together. You set examples for others to strive to serve others the best you can. This life isn't going to be easy. You may think that some people may get the easy pass, but I assure you they don't. You may have been a world-renowned singer in your last life and in this one, you're a bull rider and not a very good one. Show me what you've got! You can take it. You have Spirit Guides and angels helping you and guiding you all of the time. You have a choice of what road to take. Take the high road or the low road and you learn the same life lessons. Take a shortcut or take the long scenic route. It doesn't matter! You have an infinity of lives to get it right.

Okay, so why don't you share what you've learned with someone else so they don't have to make the same mistakes that you made? People want to learn all over the place. Go back to the lists you made. Take your "Wish List" of things you enjoy doing or would like to enjoy doing and combine it with the second list, the "Happy List." Wow, you have a potential life purpose. I loved getting readings by mediums that brought through my close friends and relatives on the other side. I studied for six years to get good enough to give outstanding readings that could change someone's life or get them back on their life path. I can and do help teach and train other mediums, because it's my life's purpose, at least, at this time in my life.

What can you do to change the world for the better? What can you do to help someone find their path? Make another list if you want. (You can see I'm into lists.) What if you are a bartender and make the best margarita in the world. Margaritas can make people happy. You could teach others to make the best margarita! You see were I'm going with this! You can speak English? There are millions of people wanting to learn. You can read? There are millions wanting to learn how to read? You can tie your shoes? There are millions of small children willing to learn! Get off your butt and take names and kick ass! (an old cowboy saying). What are you waiting for? Teach, serve and evolve! Oh, by the way, the hardest thing about helping other people with their lives is that you can't judge! That may be a major obstacle for some people. No hating and no judging. Everyone on this Earth is here for a reason. That reason is to develop, grow and evolve with their life and soul lessons. All of the stuff you can't learn in heaven and the other side is here. Don't judge!

GUIDING LIGHT

Spirit Guides serve us, because in helping us they serve our great Creator. In return, our happiness and peace contributes to the happiness and peace of the world.
—Sonia Choquette

You don't think that God would send his children down to Earth School without some supervision do you? I know the world seems chaotic and random at times, but trust me; you have an army of unseen helpers waiting to guide you. All you need to do is ask!

When you come down to this harsh environment that we call Earth, you have a plan. This plan is a list of adventures that you would like to experience to evolve your soul. You know the opposite of black is white because you can see them. How do you describe love to someone who has not experienced it? How do you sympathize with someone with a broken heart if you have never felt what it's like to have your heart broken? How can you experience the highs without having experienced the lows? I know: let's put it on a "life list" of things you need to experience to evolve your soul.

Oh, there are other things that need to happen to make the list complete. In a past life I did something really bad to someone in our Soul Group, so karmic law dictates that the person do something to me to equal out the karma. Karma refers to the universal law of cause and effect. Karma is created not only by physical action but also by thoughts and words. You get what you give. We reap what we sow. If not in this lifetime, then the next or the next.

How are you going to keep up with all of this information on your mission to Earth School? How about the buddy system? You make a deal with someone who is far wiser than you are and has gone through many Earth incarnations to keep up with all of this information and point you or nudge you in the right direction to learn these lessons. We'll call this person a guide. You don't want someone hanging around all of the time and getting in the way and bumping into other people's guides, so let this guide stay in spirit. We'll call them Spirit Guides. Ever wonder how you got that thought? Where do your ideas come from? Oh please, stop taking credit for things that your ego says you thought up all by yourself. After meeting your guide, you may wonder if you ever had an original idea or thought in your life! However, remember, we do have free will.

Your guide may give you an idea or point you in the right direction, but you don't have to do it. You scripted your life before you came down here with the help of many wise people on the other side. However, that doesn't mean you have to follow your own script. I've given my guides tons of headaches because my ego told me I could be selfish and hateful if I wanted to. It's my God given right! Why take the easy road when the difficult road is so much more trouble?

Does it build character to have your ass kicked so many times? It might be part of the script. Here is the best part; you can also ask to learn your life lesson in love and beauty. You don't have to physically and mentally experience all of the bad things you signed up for. You can watch someone else going through these trials and feel compassion and sorrow for them. It's that simple. Open your heart, let go of ego and ask for help!

Your guides and angels are here to help you and protect you. They are here to help you cross off the many life lessons you listed before you came down here. There is no chance. You will experience the lessons you signed up for, one way or the other. It was not by chance that you were born on a particular day and it won't be chance when you die on a particular day. Now you may choose the way you die, but it won't happen until it is your time. So it is written!

You will meet your Soul Mate or Soul Mates at the time you planned. Nothing is left to chance. Faith allows you to believe that God cares about you and has a system in place (as chaotic as it may seem) to take care of you. You have a Master Guide who stays with you throughout your entire life. Birth to death, 24/7 they are always with you. When you're ready to learn, your Master Guide may call upon other guides to help you. You may have six or seven guides helping you at any given moment. Need to learn how to hit a curve ball? Your Master Guide is calling someone out of the dugout to help. That's the way it works.

Your guides and loved ones on the other side are always around or can be called within an instant of a thought. Do you really want proof? Test them. I'm a skeptic and one sign isn't enough for me. I ask for signs in threes. Ask your guides to prove they are around you. Ask them to blink some lights in your house, turn the television on and off in the middle of the night, slide a book off the bookshelf and onto the floor. Ask them to play your favorite song when you get in the car. Ask them to show you any sign that won't scare you. Want to meet your guides and angels? It's easy. Take a deep breath, turn the page and raise your awareness!

OPENING UP

All things appear but we cannot see the gate from which they came. All men value the knowledge of what they know, but really do not know. Only those who fall back upon what knowledge cannot know really know.
—Lao Tse

Everyone is psychic! Feel it, hear it, see it and know it. It's so easy! You just have to unlearn how you hid the psychic skills you were born with. Everyone is born psychic. Just like everyone is born with artistic and athletic skills. Some are naturals and others, like me, practice every day to become better. Women are usually more open to their psychic skills than men are. It's okay to have women's intuition. Basically, you are just tuning in to your own energy and deciding how you feel about different people, places and decisions. Everything you do and every object has energy or a vibration like a radio or television wave. You can't destroy energy!

Everyone has had something psychic happen to them. Remember the time you thought about a person and shortly thereafter, they called you on the phone? Coincidence or chance? There is no such thing as a coincidence! Everything happens for a reason and everything is synchronistic. Remember when you had bad feelings about someone you just met and later, you learned that you were right? That's using your psychic skills or intuition. Call it what you want, but you have it. Why would you deny it? You started denying it around age five or six. This is when you began to listen to people older than you who have always done things the hard way. You do what they want and you get a reward. You go your own way and you get punished.

It's time to recover those lost skills. It is the easiest thing you will ever do. You just have to notice how you are feeling and how you are getting your information. First, you need to understand how you receive information without the use of your five senses. There are six other senses that your mind uses:

Clairvoyance literally means clear seeing. This is the ability to see things in your mind's eye. When you shut your eyes and think of someone, you can see that person in your mind. Clairvoyants can see the images in the mind's eye as a movie or a still photograph. Often, your Spirit Guide will choose this way to communicate with you by giving you information, by flashing words, like on a chalkboard in your mind's eye. Eyes open or eyes shut, your mind interprets the information the same way.

Clairaudience is Clear Hearing. Think of someone calling your name. Maybe it is your mother calling you when you got into trouble. You literally hear something in your head. Your Spirit Guides will use this inner voice to talk to you through your thoughts. Your soul or Higher Self communicates this way with you. The dead talk to me using their voices or mine.

Claircognizance is Clear Knowing. This is the gut

feeling you get when you just know something. You don't know how you got it, you just know. A claircognizant feeling is a feeling of clear certainty. The information pops into your head as if it were a memory. However, you don't remember learning the information in a conventional way. If you hear a song, your mind goes, "Oh yeah! I remember when I first heard that on the radio." With claircognizance you won't be able to remember, just that you have the information. Trust what you know that you know.

Clairsentience is Clear Sensing. This is when you can feel the emotions or pain someone felt or is feeling. You may feel what a person is feeling when they are feeling a particular sensation or emotion. This happens to empathetic people. The pain or discomfort you are feeling may not be yours, but the person you are talking to, or it could be someone else you know who is close to you, and you are feeling the same feelings through time and space. It's just like walking up to someone and you instantly feel sad. You are picking up on this person's emotions.

Clairalience is Clear Smelling. You will be able to get

all kinds of smells including perfumes, foods, etc. Scent is very powerful in our memories and scents can connect us to emotions. Why do you smell smoke when there is no fire around you? What are your guides, angels or soul trying to say to you?

Clairambience is Clear Tasting: This is the ability to receive tastes without tasting something in your mouth. Do you taste something metallic in your mind? Is the person you are talking to going through chemotherapy?

You are now aware of six additional senses you can use to your own advantage. You will use these senses to become more aware of the people and places around you. You are opening up your awareness. Smell rain and it rains later. Is this a coincidence? Not hardly. So, when the thought appears in your mind that it may rain and you don't know where it came from, don't ignore it. Grab an umbrella, because there are no coincidences!

Using these newfound senses will also be helpful in getting information from the past. Psychometry is the physical act of touching or holding an object and receiving information about the object or anyone who was associated with it. I can hold a ring that belonged to someone and get information about the person who wore it. This involves using my psychic skills to connect and read the energy left on the ring. I may be able to see images of the owner, or details of what the owner of the ring was doing as he wore the ring. Everything you do and every object has a vibration or energy. Remember: you can't destroy energy.

To experience these other senses of the mind, all you have to do is to be open to them. Welcome back these senses, just like old friends who guided you as a baby, toddler and little person. That is, until you developed an ego that was shaped by an environment that you had no control over. It's time to take back your life. Use everything that you have to make your life better and to make better the lives of the people around you. To help open up, I recommend learning how to raise your vibration or energy level. The spiritualist's call this "sitting in the power." I call it getting into your zone!

As a medium, I raise my energy to talk to those on the other side. I can also raise it to see what is going on with other people who are living. I'm a psychic when I'm using the energy to find out what is going on with people's lives and a medium when communicating to dead people. As a medium, I must raise my vibrations and the spirit must lower theirs to make a connection. I used to think this was a 50-50 proposition. Now I think it's more 95% with the spirit and 5% from the medium. It is a very hard five percent to develop! You are going to raise your energy and vibrations just 5% to help you find your way in the world and take full advantage of your consciousness. Your Higher Self or soul raises vibrations every night and leaves your body when you're asleep. So, it's not as if your body doesn't know what it's doing. You just have to train your brain to do it while you are awake.

When I say "raise your vibrations," I'm really talking about raising your consciousness and awareness. Basically, you're moving your mental process to a higher plane, while you're still grounded on the Earth plane. There are many exercises to help you develop this.

You receive most of your information in three places at the top of your body. These locations on your body are called chakras, which are spinning wheels of energy in your body. These are the "life forces" of your body and stay with the soul. The top three chakras are located at the throat, third eye (forehead) and crown (a point just above the head). This is where you want your consciousness to reside. Think of yourself sitting in a chair with your feet in a warm bucket of water. The water starts rising up into your body, traveling up your feet, legs, torso chest, neck, and head and then to a place just above your head. That is where you want your energy. Think about the center of your forehead. Now your attention is on your third eye. Then, raise your attention to just above your head. Now, you are in your crown chakra. You're raising this energy with your mind.

Pete Sanders Jr. calls this a "soul shift," the spiritualists call it "sitting in the power," and me, I'm in the zone. Have you ever started daydreaming while you were driving and don't remember driving past certain landmarks you are used to seeing and all of a sudden your perception changes and you're in the current moment? What happened to that moment in real time? Sometimes it's scary. Why didn't you wreck the car? Because your Higher Self or soul was driving the car while you were out running around in space. When you daydream or raise your vibration, your right side of the brain and creative side is taking over. Your left side of the brain is driving the car, while your soul carefully watches you. Have you ever skipped moments in time? Taken a trip and didn't know where you went or how you got back? Experienced déjà vu? It's all an energy trip. Just experience the vibrations as you do when you listen to the radio or watch television. It's your mind that reacts to the visions from the television program that you're watching. The mind reacts based on past experiences and choices you made or were made for you about how to react; such as pleasure or revulsion. It's really simple if you think about it. Remember a song you first heard long ago. Does the song bring back memories of what you were doing, where you were living, who was around you? How does that happen? Those memories are triggered by the song. They still exist because they are energy and energy can't be destroyed. Science can prove it all. You don't need to know how it works to use it. I don't need to know how to build a radio to use it. I don't need to construct a song and know where it came from to enjoy the vibrations of sound and voice!

When you are in an awakened state, your awareness is all around you even though you don't know it. Unconsciously you are in some type of power that you can't explain. Open your mind and make an effort to collect information from all of your senses and the senses in your mind. That's all you have to do! You think it and it happens. You don't have to think to pick up a glass of water and yet you do. It's freaking amazing! It's so simple, but you haven't had to think about doing something like that since you were very young, so it seems strange. Feel the energy around you. Are you happy or sad? Either way, it is a state of mind. Energy surrounds you at every given moment. So tap into that energy and experience it. Your mind has thousands of bits of information coming to it at any given moment. Did you forget to breathe? Of course not. Your mind is taking care of it. Does the back of your hand itch? How did you know? Why did your mind bring this information to the front of your consciousness? It must be important. Now, retrain your mind to understand what is important to you.

You want to empower your mind to take advantage of the senses you are not currently using to help you and your soul to evolve. Ego doesn't like to be ignored. Release the ego, the doubts, and enjoy what you've been missing. You are on a rollercoaster of life so enjoy it! This isn't an out-of-body experience. It's like watching a television show turn from black and white to color. It's tuning the bass and treble on your sound system to hear the sounds you were meant to hear from the artist of the music.

There are many guided meditations to help you raise your vibrations and start experiencing your other senses. Take a deep breath and you just increased your energy level. Now what are you going to do with it?

JUST BREATHE

Man's heart away from nature becomes hard.
—Standing Bear

Think about a time when you were completely relaxed and had a moment of clarity. Everything made sense and you were at peace with yourself and the world. That is what meditation is all about. Forget what you've seen on television or heard from someone who hasn't ever meditated. Meditation is about taking a time out for your mind and soul to heal. It helps your soul or spiritual side to develop to its full potential.

Meditation can sharpen your other senses, including your sixth sense and increase awareness in your body, mind and spirit. It awakens you to the present moment and allows you to focus your life. You'll understand what matters most and put your life in perspective. What do you want to achieve? What stands in your way? Meditate on it and get clarity.

Meditation teaches us how to center ourselves and our thoughts. Jack Kornfield says "The spirit you will need to bring to meditation is one of openness, of discovery, of seeing. To sit, to walk and to train yourself to bring your attention back to the present moment. To learn how to concentrate mindfully in a balanced way and to observe your breath, your body, your emotions and your mind."

I recommend that you research different techniques on meditation. Get a book about meditation and listen to some guided meditations. The meditation is like a staircase, taking you to the top of a mountain to raise your vibrations. It all starts with you using your breath to open up energetically and mentally channeling that energy for your purpose and needs.

Breath work is as important to opening your

psychic senses as it is to an Olympic athlete in training. Your body receives energy from the food you eat and the air you breathe. Air fuels the fire and raises your vibrations. You must raise your vibrations to experience more of the world around you. It also helps with peace of mind.

If it was easy, everyone could do it. It is easy, but it takes a lot of work and practice, just like anything else you want to be good at. A baby has the most efficient breathing method. They breathe from deep in the bottom of their lungs with such ease. Most of us breathe from the top part of our lungs and don't get the full benefit of the air available to our brains and body. Want to increase your energy, become healthier and connect to the spirit? Re-learn how to breathe.

We aren't accustomed to using the muscles connected to our diaphragm and lower lungs to breathe. You have to stretch them out and work them out. Try lying on the floor in a comfortable position and placing your hand on your lower abdomen to feel how you are breathing. Now take a deep breath. See how the air fills the top of your lungs first? Now expand your abdominal muscles and breathe from the lower part of your lungs first and continue until all of your lungs are full of air. This is the goal in breathing to get the most energy for your body and mind. Like any under-developed muscle, if you practice too much, they will become sore. It's easier to practice lying on your back at this point than sitting in a chair.

There are different ways to breathe. Inhaling through your nose and exhaling through your mouth are most beneficial to mediumship and psychic work. While doing this, also place the tip of your tongue to the top of your mouth just behind your teeth. This will aid in making connections. It is similar to mudras in yoga (different ways of holding your fingers and hands to aid energy connections.) It's all about getting the biggest energy bang for your buck. Energy helps you connect to your Higher Self and soul. While meditating, practice your breath work. This too becomes a trigger for your psychic skills. Practice taking three or four pranic breaths before you raise your energy and rise into your zone.

Another trigger for your meditation and transformation are scents. Scents from candles or incense can help raise your vibrations and get you into the zone.

Incense has been enjoyed in its natural form since ancient times. It can calm, relax and energize you and make it easier to induce meditative states. Scent triggers memories that can take you back to the past in a gentle way. A scent can remind you of other pleasures and set the scene for meaningful, reflective moments.

Incense, resins and botanicals are still used today in various Native American, metaphysical and religious ceremonies and rituals to promote the state of mind necessary to raise and direct personal energy. Some fragrances can purify a room of negative vibrations. Incense is used for meditation or for simply scenting a room. The aromatherapy of scent can be used by burning candles, incense, resins and herbs. You can burn herbs in their raw form by placing them on top of burning charcoal tablets. The ancient Chinese believed that different scents induced different reactions such as tranquility and peaceful solitude.

IMAGINE

There is no thought in any mind, but it quickly tends to convert itself into power.

—Emerson

Imagination will be one of the most important tools in transforming your life. If you can imagine where you want to be, who you want to be and gather the incredible good feelings around these thoughts and images, your life will be changed forever! All you need is a target. You've made your lists and decided what you want to do, how you want to transform your life and find your path! Now visualize this transformation. You have to think it and own it. You must know how good it will feel. Remember not to lose focus about the journey to get there. It's all about the journey! Sure, it will feel good to make a goal. However, it's how you get there that is the story of your life lessons.

The brain doesn't know the difference between a dream and reality. When you are having a dream, your mind thinks that it is real. You create the emotions and feelings that are so real that it actually raises your heart rate and gets your body to move. That's great! We can trick the brain so it doesn't know we can't catch the game-winning touchdown or become the James Bond of our dreams, creating and doing the impossible.

I want to be the quarterback for the Dallas Cowboys and take them to the Super Bowl and win it! However, that doesn't mean I have the equipment to do it. I'm about the right height and weight for a quarterback. I just don't have the legs and arms necessary to run and throw. You have to imagine realistically. I have a degree in journalism from college and could cover the Super Bowl for Sports Illustrated. The dream becomes a little more realistic.

Great golfers visualize how they are going to hit the ball on a certain course. They practice the visualization over and over, until they can see it, feel it and know it. They imagine so much so that the little neurons making paths in the brain, train the brain that it's already happened. We can trick the brain! Martial arts masters can visualize the forms of their art in their mind and it is as if they are actually doing it to the mind. Repetition of thought makes it so. If someone tells you that you are ugly all of your life, you would start to believe it. Someone else may have put limitations on you and your brain has heard it over and over again and believes it. Maybe you have put the limitations on yourself!

You were born with a special set of skills. With these skills and the help of your guides and angels, you can experience what you were meant to experience in this lifetime. I can be quarterback in another lifetime. In this lifetime, I was meant to be a medium, to help people work through their losses and grief to get them back on their path! I feel good about it; the client feels better, knowing there is no death and their loved ones are always around them. I get to work off a hell of a lot of karma and maybe pay it forward. It took a while for me to come to this conclusion and accept my gifts through an accident, but I know it's my destiny.

What's your destiny? You start to build your reality in your mind. We've already been over what you like, what makes you happy, what you're grateful for and what you could do for others. Now, put it all together and imagine the life you were meant to live! It starts out as a thought, but you have the energy to transform it to reality. Positive energy attracts positive energy. Attract what you want in your life, not what you don't want. It may not seem like much but it makes a big difference to your mind. It's like trying to get an annoying song out of your head. Think about it and it won't go away. Replace it with a song you want to hear and you hear that song. Don't worry about anything. Leave any worrying to your guides. They can handle it.

Use a trigger to help bring up the reality that you want. Pick a favorite song and use the song in the mix of your visualization. Are you climbing Mt. Everest? Then have your earphones on as you're climbing the mountain and it's playing your song, "Don't Stop Believing." Every time you hear that song on the radio, use it as a trigger or tool to motivate you. Then you think about how every muscle feels in your body climbing the mountain, the breath leaving your mouth, the thrill and confidence you have as you climb step by step. You hear your favorite music and it motivates you to carry on! What does it feel like to make it to the summit? Are your muscles aching? Are you short of breath? Do you literally feel that you are on top of the world? Remember the feelings, the weather, the atmosphere, how your clothes fit and boots feel; envision it all!

Olympic gold medalist swimmer, Jon Naber, visualized himself standing on the gold medal stand with the gold medal hanging around his neck, the sound of the National Anthem and a stocking cap on his head! He kept that cap in the top drawer of his chest of drawers and took the hat out to wear often. He created the feelings, the atmosphere, and moisture in the air, the cheering crowd, how great it felt to touch the wall first! You can do the same. Envision often and recreate your goals in your mind. Your mind doesn't know the difference, so at the right time, you ask yourself and your body to complete your goal. The mind has already done this hundreds of times and the reality is just one more time! It's a piece of cake!

Just remember a thought is energy! Want more proof? The placebo effect. Look it up. The mind is so powerful that if you tell a patient that you are giving them a pill that will cure their ailment and the ailment is cured, even though the patient was given a placebo or sugar pill. The mind thought it would cure, so it did! That is so powerful. Your mind controls your body and actions and now you can control your mind. You can place positive and active thoughts in your mind that you want to be true, that you have already imagined to be true and your mind will create the opportunities to make your wishes and dreams come true!

In this lifetime you will live, learn and love. As

you progress in this life, you will serve, teach and evolve. It is a never-ending circle. As you live, you will serve others. As you learn, you will also teach. As you love, you begin to evolve. The cycle never ends. The more you evolve the more cycles occur in your lifetime. You can have one slow cycle in your lifetime or you can move on as fast as you can ascend and graduate from your life lessons and begin to understand the laws of the universe.

You are sitting down at the crossroads. Get off your butt and dust yourself off! Think about what you want to happen in your life and make it happen. Start today; it's your destiny!

STEVE SPUR

RECOMMENDED READING

(Listed by year published)

The Story of Edgar Cayce, by Thomas Sugrue, 1942

Illusions, by Richard Bach, 1977

Zen in the Martial Arts, by Joe Hyams, 1979

Many Lives, Many Masters, by Brian Weiss, 1988

Journey of Awakening, by Ram Dass, 1990

You Are Psychic, by Pete Sanders Jr., 1990

Grandfather, by Tom Brown Jr., 1993

Journey of Souls, by Michael Newton, 1994

Children's Past Lives, by Carol Bowman, 1997

Talking to Heaven, by James Van Praagh, 1997

One Last Time, by John Edward, 1998

Crossing Over, by John Edward, 2001

The After Life Experiments, by Gary Schwartz, PhD., 2002

Spirit Messenger, by Gordon Smith, 2004

Don't Kiss Them Good-Bye, by Allison DuBois, 2005

The Secret, by Rhonda Byrne, 2006

ABOUT THE AUTHOR

Steve Spur is an evidential medium based in Dallas, Texas. He connects people all over the world with their loved ones in spirit to bring messages of love and hope. He proves they are alive and well on the other side.

He is a cowboy who was raised in West Texas and worked as a bartender, bouncer and with horses for over 15 years until an accident gave him his psychic gifts of clairvoyance (clear seeing) and clairaudience (clear hearing). He was a skeptic and didn't believe in God or an afterlife until the accident changed his life forever.

He now devotes his life to prove in the words of Chief Seattle, "There is no death, only a change of worlds." He teaches about the fascinating and incredible world that awaits us on the other side and that everything you do in this lifetime will make a difference in the next.

www.cowboypsychic.com

www.ingramcontent.com/pod-product-compliance
Lightning Source LLC
Chambersburg PA
CBHW071412040426
42444CB00009B/2216